# Unpacking Diffusion: A Developer's Guide To Working With Diffusion Models

Written By Richard Aragon

## Table of Contents

## Chapter 1: Introduction to Diffusion Models

What are diffusion models?

Diffusion models are a type of generative model that are trained to generate data by gradually removing noise from an image or text. They are a powerful tool for generating realistic and diverse data, and they have been used for a variety of applications, including image generation, text generation, and natural language processing.

Diffusion models work by starting with a noisy image or text and then gradually removing the noise. At each step, the model predicts the next step in the diffusion process, and the predicted image or text is then used as the input for the next step. This process continues until the model reaches the desired level of detail.

1

There are several different types of diffusion models, but they all share the same basic principle. The most common type of diffusion model is the Bayesian diffusion model. Bayesian diffusion models are trained using a Bayesian framework, which means that they take into account the uncertainty in the data. This makes them more robust to noise and outliers than other types of diffusion models.

Diffusion models have a number of advantages over other types of generative models. They are able to generate realistic and diverse data, and they are relatively easy to train. However, they also have some limitations. They can be slow to train, and they can be sensitive to the choice of hyperparameters.

Despite their limitations, diffusion models are a powerful tool for generating data. They are likely to become increasingly popular in the future, as they are used for a wider range of applications.

Here are some of the applications of diffusion models:

- Image generation: Diffusion models can be used to generate realistic images of faces, objects, and scenes.
- Text generation: Diffusion models can be used to generate realistic text, such as news articles, poems, and code.
- Natural language processing: Diffusion models can be used for a variety of natural language processing tasks, such as machine translation and text summarization.
- Data augmentation: Diffusion models can be used to augment data sets by generating new data points that are similar to the existing data points. This can be useful for training machine learning models.

## How do diffusion models work?

Diffusion models are a type of generative model that are trained to generate data by gradually removing noise from an image or text. They work by starting with a noisy image or text and then gradually removing the noise. At each step, the model predicts the next step in the diffusion process, and the predicted image or text is then used as the input for the next step. This process continues until the model reaches the desired level of detail.

Here is a more detailed explanation of how diffusion models work:

1. The model is first trained on a dataset of images or text. The training data is typically noisy, so the model learns to remove the noise and generate realistic images or text.
2. Once the model is trained, it can be used to generate new images or text. The process of generating new data is called inference.
3. To generate new data, the model starts with a noisy image or text. Then, at each step, the model predicts the next step in the diffusion process. The predicted image or text is then used as the input for the next step.
4. This process continues until the model reaches the desired level of detail. The final image or text will be a realistic image or text that is free of noise.

Here is an example of how a diffusion model can be used to generate an image:

1. The model is trained on a dataset of images of cats.
2. The model is then used to generate a new image of a cat. The model starts with a noisy image of a cat.
3. At each step, the model predicts the next step in the diffusion process. The predicted image is then used as the input for the next step.
4. This process continues until the model reaches the desired level of detail. The final image will be a realistic image of a cat that is free of noise.

Diffusion models are a powerful tool for generating realistic and diverse data. They are relatively easy to train, and they can be used for a variety of applications. However, they can be slow to train, and they can be sensitive to the choice of hyperparameters.

## The different types of diffusion models

Diffusion models are a type of generative model that are trained to generate data by gradually removing noise from an image or text. There are several different types of diffusion models, but they all share the same basic principle.
The most common type of diffusion model is the Bayesian diffusion model.
Bayesian diffusion models are trained using a Bayesian framework, which means

that they take into account the uncertainty in the data. This makes them more robust to noise and outliers than other types of diffusion models.
Other types of diffusion models include:

- Non-Bayesian diffusion models: These models do not use a Bayesian framework. They are typically less robust to noise and outliers than Bayesian diffusion models, but they can be faster to train.
- Score-based diffusion models: These models use a score function to measure the quality of a generated image or text. The model is then trained to maximize the score function.
- Stochastic diffusion models: These models use stochastic noise to generate images or text. This makes them more diverse than deterministic diffusion models, but it can also make them less stable.

The choice of diffusion model depends on the specific application. Bayesian diffusion models are typically the most robust and versatile, but they can be slow to train. Non-Bayesian diffusion models are faster to train, but they can be less robust to noise. Score-based diffusion models are a good compromise between robustness and speed. Stochastic diffusion models are a good choice for applications that require diversity.
Here are some of the benefits and limitations of different types of diffusion models:

- Bayesian diffusion models:

    - Benefits: More robust to noise and outliers, more versatile
    - Limitations: Slow to train

- Non-Bayesian diffusion models:

    - Benefits: Faster to train
    - Limitations: Less robust to noise and outliers

- Score-based diffusion models:

- Benefits: Can be more diverse than deterministic diffusion models
  - Limitations: Can be less stable

- Stochastic diffusion models:

  - Benefits: Can be more diverse than deterministic diffusion models
  - Limitations: Can be less stable

# The benefits and limitations of diffusion models

Diffusion models are a type of generative model that are trained to generate data by gradually removing noise from an image or text. They have a number of benefits and limitations.
Benefits:

- Can generate realistic and diverse data: Diffusion models can generate realistic and diverse data, including images, text, and other types of data.
- Relatively easy to train: Diffusion models are relatively easy to train, compared to other types of generative models.
- Can be used for a variety of applications: Diffusion models can be used for a variety of applications, including image generation, text generation, and natural language processing.

Limitations:

- Can be slow to train: Diffusion models can be slow to train, especially for large datasets.
- Can be sensitive to the choice of hyperparameters: The performance of diffusion models can be sensitive to the choice of hyperparameters, such as the amount of noise to be removed at each step.
- Can generate artifacts: Diffusion models can sometimes generate artifacts, such as blurry edges or unnatural patterns.

Overall, diffusion models are a powerful tool for generating data. They are relatively easy to train and can be used for a variety of applications. However, they can be slow to train and can be sensitive to the choice of hyperparameters.
Here are some of the ways to mitigate the limitations of diffusion models:

- Use a larger dataset: Using a larger dataset can help to improve the performance of diffusion models.
- Use a better optimization algorithm: Using a better optimization algorithm can help to speed up the training process.
- Tune the hyperparameters: Carefully tuning the hyperparameters can help to improve the performance of diffusion models.
- Use a post-processing step: A post-processing step can be used to remove artifacts from generated data.

## Potential use cases of diffusion models beyond image generation

Diffusion models are a type of generative model that are trained to generate data by gradually removing noise from an image or text. They have been used for a variety of applications, including image generation, text generation, and natural language processing.
However, diffusion models can also be used for other purposes, such as:

- Data augmentation: Diffusion models can be used to augment data sets by generating new data points that are similar to the existing data points. This can be useful for training machine learning models.
- Image restoration: Diffusion models can be used to restore images that have been corrupted by noise or blur.
- Text generation: Diffusion models can be used to generate text, such as news articles, poems, and code.
- Natural language processing: Diffusion models can be used for a variety of natural language processing tasks, such as machine translation and text summarization.

- Software security: Diffusion models can be used to generate synthetic code that is similar to real code. This can be used to train machine learning models to detect malware or other security vulnerabilities.

Here is a more detailed explanation of some of these potential use cases:

- Data augmentation: Data augmentation is a technique used to increase the size and diversity of a data set. This can be done by artificially creating new data points that are similar to the existing data points. Diffusion models can be used to generate new data points that are similar to the existing data points in a data set. This can be useful for training machine learning models, as it can help to prevent the models from overfitting to the training data.
- Image restoration: Image restoration is the process of restoring an image that has been corrupted by noise or blur. Diffusion models can be used to restore images by gradually removing the noise or blur. This can be useful for recovering images that have been damaged by compression, digitization, or other processes.
- Text generation: Diffusion models can be used to generate text, such as news articles, poems, and code. This can be useful for a variety of purposes, such as creating content for websites or generating creative text formats.
- Natural language processing: Diffusion models can be used for a variety of natural language processing tasks, such as machine translation and text summarization. Machine translation is the process of translating text from one language to another. Diffusion models can be used to generate synthetic text that is similar to real text. This can be used to train machine learning models to translate text from one language to another. Text summarization is the process ofcondensing a piece of text into a shorter and more concise version. Diffusion models can be used to generate synthetic text that is similar to real text. This can be used to train machine learning models to summarize text.
- Software security: Diffusion models can be used to generate synthetic code that is similar to real code. This can be used to train machine learning models to detect malware or other security vulnerabilities. Malware is software that is designed to harm a computer system. Diffusion models can be used to generate synthetic malware that is similar to real malware. This can be used to train machine learning models to detect malware.

These are just a few of the potential use cases of diffusion models beyond image generation. As diffusion models continue to develop, it is likely that they will be used for even more applications.

# Chapter 2: Data Preparation for Diffusion Models

## The types of data that can be used for diffusion models

Diffusion models are a type of generative model that are trained to generate data by gradually removing noise from an image or text. They can be used to generate a variety of data types, including:

- Images: Diffusion models can be used to generate realistic images of faces, objects, and scenes.
- Text: Diffusion models can be used to generate realistic text, such as news articles, poems, and code.
- Audio: Diffusion models can be used to generate realistic audio recordings, such as music and speech.
- Video: Diffusion models can be used to generate realistic videos, such as movies and TV shows.
- 3D models: Diffusion models can be used to generate realistic 3D models, such as sculptures and buildings.
- Time series data: Diffusion models can be used to generate time series data, such as stock prices and weather data.

The type of data that can be used for diffusion models depends on the specific model. Some models are better suited for generating images, while others are better suited for generating text.

The data that is used to train a diffusion model should be representative of the data that the model will be used to generate. For example, if a diffusion model is being trained to generate images of cats, the training data should include a variety of images of cats.

The quality of the data that is used to train a diffusion model will affect the quality of the generated data. If the data is noisy or low-quality, the generated data will also be noisy or low-quality.

Here are some of the considerations when choosing the data to use for diffusion models:

- Representativeness: The data should be representative of the data that the model will be used to generate.
- Quality: The data should be high-quality and free of noise.
- Size: The data should be large enough to train the model.
- Variety: The data should be varied to help the model learn to generate different types of data.

## Data preprocessing for diffusion models

Diffusion models are a type of generative model that are trained to generate data by gradually removing noise from an image or text. The quality of the generated data depends on the quality of the data that is used to train the model. Therefore, it is important to pre-process the data before training the model.

The data preprocessing steps for diffusion models vary depending on the type of data that is being used. However, some common data preprocessing steps include:

- Image resizing: Images are typically resized to a fixed size before training the model. This helps to speed up the training process and improve the performance of the model.
- Image normalization: Images are typically normalized to have zero mean and unit variance. This helps to improve the stability of the training process.
- Text cleaning: Text is typically cleaned to remove noise, such as punctuation, stop words, and other unwanted characters. This helps to improve the performance of the model.
- Text tokenization: Text is typically tokenized into words or phrases. This helps the model to learn the relationships between different words and phrases.

In addition to these common data preprocessing steps, there are a number of other steps that can be taken to improve the quality of the generated data. These steps may include:

- Data augmentation: Data augmentation is the process of artificially creating new data points from existing data points. This can be done by applying transformations, such as rotation, cropping, and flipping. Data augmentation helps to improve the diversity of the training data and can help to prevent the model from overfitting.
- Data sampling: Data sampling is the process of selecting a subset of the data to use for training the model. This can be done to reduce the size of the training data or to focus on a specific subset of the data. Data sampling can help to improve the efficiency of the training process and can help to improve the performance of the model.

The specific data preprocessing steps that are used will depend on the specific diffusion model and the type of data that is being used. However, the steps described above are a good starting point for most diffusion models.

## Generating training data for diffusion models

Diffusion models are a type of generative model that are trained to generate data by gradually removing noise from an image or text. The quality of the generated data depends on the quality of the training data. Therefore, it is important to generate high-quality training data for diffusion models.
The process of generating training data for diffusion models varies depending on the type of data that is being used. However, some common methods for generating training data for diffusion models include:

- Collecting and annotating data: This involves collecting a large dataset of images or text and annotating the data with labels. The labels can be used to train the diffusion model to generate specific types of data.

- Generating synthetic data: This involves using a computer program to generate artificial data that is similar to the real data. Synthetic data can be useful for training diffusion models when it is difficult or expensive to collect real data.
- Transfer learning: This involves using a pre-trained diffusion model to generate training data for a new diffusion model. Transfer learning can be useful for speeding up the training process and improving the performance of the new diffusion model.

The specific method for generating training data for diffusion models will depend on the specific diffusion model and the type of data that is being used. However, the methods described above are a good starting point for most diffusion models. Here are some additional tips for generating training data for diffusion models:

- Use a variety of data: The training data should be varied to help the model learn to generate different types of data.
- Label the data carefully: The labels should be accurate and consistent to help the model learn to generate the desired data.
- Use a large dataset: A large dataset will help the model learn to generate more realistic data.
- Use a good quality dataset: The dataset should be high-quality and free of noise to help the model learn to generate high-quality data.

# Chapter 3: Constructing Diffusion Models

## The different components of a diffusion model

Diffusion models are a type of generative model that are trained to generate data by gradually removing noise from an image or text. They are composed of several different components, including:

- The noise: The noise is the random data that is used to initialize the diffusion model. The noise can be generated using a variety of methods, such as Gaussian noise or uniform noise.
- The diffusion process: The diffusion process is the process of gradually removing the noise from the image or text. The diffusion process is typically implemented as a neural network.
- The decoder: The decoder is the model that is used to reconstruct the image or text from the latent representation. The decoder is typically implemented as a neural network.
- The hyperparameters: The hyperparameters are the settings of the diffusion model, such as the learning rate and the number of steps in the diffusion process. The hyperparameters are typically tuned to optimize the performance of the model.

The different components of a diffusion model work together to generate data. The noise is used to initialize the diffusion process, and the diffusion process gradually removes the noise from the image or text. The decoder is then used to reconstruct the image or text from the latent representation.

The specific components of a diffusion model can vary depending on the specific model. However, the components described above are common to most diffusion models.

Here are some additional details about the different components of a diffusion model:

- The noise: The noise is used to initialize the diffusion process. The noise can be generated using a variety of methods, such as Gaussian noise or uniform noise. The choice of noise distribution will affect the quality of the generated data.
- The diffusion process: The diffusion process is the process of gradually removing the noise from the image or text. The diffusion process is typically implemented as a neural network. The diffusion process is typically iterated over a number of steps, and the noise is gradually removed at each step.
- The decoder: The decoder is the model that is used to reconstruct the image or text from the latent representation. The decoder is typically implemented as a neural network. The decoder takes the latent representation as input and outputs the image or text.
- The hyperparameters: The hyperparameters are the settings of the diffusion model, such as the learning rate and the number of steps in the diffusion process. The hyperparameters are typically tuned to optimize the performance of the model.

The choice of hyperparameters can have a significant impact on the performance of the diffusion model. The learning rate controls the amount of updates that are made to the model parameters during training. The number of steps in the diffusion process controls how much noise is removed from the image or text.

## The hyperparameters of a diffusion model

Diffusion models are a type of generative model that are trained to generate data by gradually removing noise from an image or text. The hyperparameters of a diffusion model are the settings of the model, such as the learning rate and the number of steps in the diffusion process. The hyperparameters are typically tuned to optimize the performance of the model.
The hyperparameters of a diffusion model can vary depending on the specific model. However, some common hyperparameters include:

- Learning rate: The learning rate controls the amount of updates that are made to the model parameters during training. A higher learning rate will lead to faster training, but it may also lead to instability. A lower learning rate will lead to slower training, but it may also lead to better performance.

- Number of steps: The number of steps in the diffusion process controls how much noise is removed from the image or text. A higher number of steps will lead to more realistic data, but it will also lead to longer training times.
- Noise distribution: The noise distribution controls the type of noise that is used to initialize the diffusion process. A different noise distribution will lead to different results.
- Loss function: The loss function is used to measure the quality of the generated data. A different loss function will lead to different results.
- Optimizer: The optimizer is used to update the model parameters during training. A different optimizer may lead to different results.

The choice of hyperparameters can have a significant impact on the performance of the diffusion model. The learning rate controls the amount of updates that are made to the model parameters during training. The number of steps in the diffusion process controls how much noise is removed from the image or text. The noise distribution controls the type of noise that is used to initialize the diffusion process. The loss function controls how the quality of the generated data is measured. The optimizer controls how the model parameters are updated during training.
The hyperparameters of a diffusion model can be tuned manually or automatically. Manual tuning involves trial and error, while automatic tuning involves using a search algorithm to find the best hyperparameters.

## Choosing the right diffusion model for your application

Diffusion models are a type of generative model that are trained to generate data by gradually removing noise from an image or text. There are many different diffusion models available, and the best model for your application will depend on a number of factors, including:

- The type of data you want to generate: Diffusion models can be used to generate a variety of data types, including images, text, and audio. The type of data you want to generate will determine the type of diffusion model that is best suited for your application.

- The quality of the generated data: Different diffusion models produce different levels of quality in the generated data. If you need high-quality generated data, you will need to choose a diffusion model that is known for its performance.
- The speed of training: Diffusion models can take a long time to train, especially for large datasets. If you need to train a diffusion model quickly, you will need to choose a model that is known for its efficiency.
- The availability of pre-trained models: Some diffusion models are available as pre-trained models, which can be used to generate data without having to train the model from scratch. If you need to generate data quickly, you can use a pre-trained diffusion model.

Here are some of the most popular diffusion models:

- DALL-E 2: DALL-E 2 is a diffusion model that can be used to generate realistic images from text descriptions. It is known for its high quality of generated images.
- VQGAN+CLIP: VQGAN+CLIP is a diffusion model that can be used to generate images from text descriptions or from other images. It is known for its ability to generate images that are both realistic and creative.
- BigGAN: BigGAN is a diffusion model that can be used to generate realistic images from scratch. It is known for its ability to generate images that are both realistic and diverse.
- Stable Diffusion: Stable Diffusion is a diffusion model that is known for its stability and efficiency. It is a good choice for applications where it is important to generate data quickly and reliably.

The best way to choose the right diffusion model for your application is to experiment with different models and see which one produces the best results for your specific needs.

# Chapter 4: Training Diffusion Models

## The different training methods for diffusion models

Diffusion models are a type of generative model that are trained to generate data by gradually removing noise from an image or text. There are several different training methods for diffusion models, each with its own advantages and disadvantages.

- Contrastive diffusion: Contrastive diffusion is a training method for diffusion models that uses a contrastive loss function. The contrastive loss function compares the generated data to the real data and tries to minimize the difference between them. Contrastive diffusion is a relatively simple training method, but it can be effective for generating realistic data.
- Adversarial diffusion: Adversarial diffusion is a training method for diffusion models that uses an adversarial loss function. The adversarial loss function pits a generator model against a discriminator model. The generator model tries to generate data that is indistinguishable from real data, while the discriminator model tries to distinguish between real and generated data. Adversarial diffusion can be more effective than contrastive diffusion for generating realistic data, but it can also be more difficult to train.
- Self-supervised diffusion: Self-supervised diffusion is a training method for diffusion models that uses self-supervised learning. Self-supervised learning does not require labeled data. Instead, it learns from unlabeled data by predicting the next step in a diffusion process. Self-supervised diffusion can be more efficient than supervised diffusion, but it can also be less effective for generating realistic data.
- One-shot diffusion: One-shot diffusion is a training method for diffusion models that uses a single image as input. One-shot diffusion can be used to generate images that are similar to the input image. However, it can be difficult to generate diverse images using one-shot diffusion.

The best training method for diffusion models will depend on the specific application. For example, if you need to generate realistic images, you may want to use contrastive diffusion or adversarial diffusion. If you need to generate images quickly, you may want to use self-supervised diffusion. If you need to generate images that are similar to a specific image, you may want to use one-shot diffusion. Here are some additional considerations when choosing a training method for diffusion models:

- The size of the dataset: The size of the dataset will affect the training time and the performance of the model. A larger dataset will typically lead to a better-performing model.
- The complexity of the model: The complexity of the model will affect the training time and the performance of the model. A more complex model will typically take longer to train, but it may also perform better.
- The availability of resources: The availability of resources, such as computing power and memory, will affect the choice of training method. Some training methods, such as adversarial diffusion, require more resources than others.

The best way to choose a training method for diffusion models is to experiment with different methods and see which one produces the best results for your specific needs.

## The hyperparameters of the training process

The training process of a diffusion model is controlled by a number of hyperparameters. These hyperparameters can have a significant impact on the performance of the model.
Some of the most important hyperparameters include:

- Learning rate: The learning rate controls the amount of updates that are made to the model parameters during training. A higher learning rate will lead to faster training, but it may also lead to instability. A lower learning rate will lead to slower training, but it may also lead to better performance.

- Number of steps: The number of steps in the diffusion process controls how much noise is removed from the image or text. A higher number of steps will lead to more realistic data, but it will also lead to longer training times.
- Noise distribution: The noise distribution controls the type of noise that is used to initialize the diffusion process. A different noise distribution will lead to different results.
- Loss function: The loss function is used to measure the quality of the generated data. A different loss function will lead to different results.
- Optimizer: The optimizer is used to update the model parameters during training. A different optimizer may lead to different results.

The hyperparameters of the training process can be tuned manually or automatically. Manual tuning involves trial and error, while automatic tuning involves using a search algorithm to find the best hyperparameters.

Here are some additional tips for tuning the hyperparameters of the training process:

- Start with a small learning rate: A lower learning rate will help to prevent the model from overfitting the training data.
- Gradually increase the learning rate: As the model learns, you can gradually increase the learning rate to speed up the training process.
- Use a noise distribution that matches the data: The noise distribution should be similar to the noise that is present in the data.
- Use a loss function that is appropriate for the data: The loss function should be designed to measure the quality of the generated data.
- Use an optimizer that is efficient and stable: The optimizer should be able to update the model parameters quickly and reliably.

The best way to tune the hyperparameters of the training process is to experiment with different values and see which ones produce the best results for your specific needs.

# Evaluating the performance of diffusion models

Diffusion models are a type of generative model that are trained to generate data by gradually removing noise from an image or text. The performance of a diffusion model can be evaluated using a variety of metrics, including:

- Fréchet Inception Distance (FID): The Fréchet Inception Distance (FID) is a metric that measures the similarity between the distribution of generated data and the distribution of real data. A lower FID score indicates that the generated data is more similar to the real data.
- Kernel Inception Distance (KID): The Kernel Inception Distance (KID) is a metric that is similar to the FID, but it is more robust to noise. A lower KID score indicates that the generated data is more similar to the real data.
- Structural Similarity Index (SSIM): The Structural Similarity Index (SSIM) is a metric that measures the similarity between two images. A higher SSIM score indicates that the two images are more similar.
- Human evaluation: Human evaluation is a subjective measure of the quality of the generated data. Human evaluators are typically asked to rate the generated data on a scale of 1 to 5, where 1 is the worst and 5 is the best.

The best metric for evaluating the performance of a diffusion model will depend on the specific application. For example, if you are interested in generating realistic images, you may want to use the FID or KID. If you are interested in generating images that are similar to a specific image, you may want to use the SSIM. If you are interested in generating images that are creative or interesting, you may want to use human evaluation.

Here are some additional considerations when evaluating the performance of diffusion models:

- The size of the dataset: The size of the dataset will affect the performance of the model. A larger dataset will typically lead to a better-performing model.
- The complexity of the model: The complexity of the model will also affect the performance of the model. A more complex model will typically take longer to train, but it may also perform better.

- The quality of the training data: The quality of the training data will also affect the performance of the model. A high-quality training dataset will typically lead to a better-performing model.

The best way to evaluate the performance of a diffusion model is to experiment with different metrics and see which ones produce the most meaningful results for your specific needs.

# Chapter 5: Fine-tuning Diffusion Models

## What is fine-tuning?

Fine-tuning is a technique in machine learning where a pre-trained model is fine-tuned on a specific task. The pre-trained model is typically trained on a large dataset of general data, such as images or text. The fine-tuning process involves training the model on a smaller dataset of data that is specific to the task.

The fine-tuning process typically involves adjusting the weights of the pre-trained model. The weights are the parameters that control the behavior of the model. The fine-tuning process is typically done using supervised learning, where the model is trained on a dataset of labeled data.

Fine-tuning can be used to improve the performance of a pre-trained model on a specific task. This is because the pre-trained model will already have learned the general features of the data. The fine-tuning process can then focus on learning the specific features of the task.

Fine-tuning can be used for a variety of tasks, such as image classification, natural language processing, and speech recognition.

Here are some of the benefits of fine-tuning:

- It can improve the performance of a pre-trained model on a specific task.
- It can be used to save time and resources, as it does not require training a model from scratch.
- It can be used to transfer knowledge from one task to another.

Here are some of the challenges of fine-tuning:

- It can be difficult to find a good dataset for fine-tuning.
- The fine-tuning process can be time-consuming and computationally expensive.
- The fine-tuning process can be unstable, and the model can overfit the training data.

Overall, fine-tuning is a powerful technique that can be used to improve the performance of pre-trained models on specific tasks. However, it is important to be aware of the challenges of fine-tuning before using it.

# How to fine-tune diffusion models

Diffusion models are a type of generative model that are trained to generate data by gradually removing noise from an image or text. Fine-tuning is a technique in machine learning where a pre-trained model is fine-tuned on a specific task. In the context of diffusion models, fine-tuning can be used to improve the performance of a pre-trained diffusion model on a specific task, such as generating images of a particular style or genre.
To fine-tune a diffusion model, you will need:

- A pre-trained diffusion model: There are many pre-trained diffusion models available, such as DALL-E 2 and VQGAN+CLIP.
- A dataset of data for the specific task: This dataset should be labeled, so that the model knows what it is supposed to generate.
- A fine-tuning algorithm: There are many fine-tuning algorithms available, such as Adam and SGD.

The fine-tuning process typically involves adjusting the weights of the pre-trained model. The weights are the parameters that control the behavior of the model. The fine-tuning process is typically done using supervised learning, where the model is trained on a dataset of labeled data.

The fine-tuning process can be done using a variety of techniques, including:

- Changing the hyperparameters: The hyperparameters of the diffusion model can be changed to improve the performance of the model on the specific task.
- Adding new layers: New layers can be added to the diffusion model to improve the performance of the model on the specific task.
- Transfer learning: Transfer learning can be used to transfer knowledge from a pre-trained diffusion model to a new diffusion model.

The fine-tuning process can be time-consuming and computationally expensive, but it can be a valuable way to improve the performance of a pre-trained diffusion model on a specific task.

Here are some additional tips for fine-tuning diffusion models:

- Start with a small learning rate: A lower learning rate will help to prevent the model from overfitting the training data.
- Gradually increase the learning rate: As the model learns, you can gradually increase the learning rate to speed up the fine-tuning process.
- Use a good dataset: The dataset for fine-tuning should be large and diverse.
- Use a good fine-tuning algorithm: The fine-tuning algorithm should be appropriate for the task.
- Be patient: The fine-tuning process can be time-consuming, so be patient and let the model learn.

The best way to fine-tune a diffusion model is to experiment with different techniques and see which ones produce the best results for your specific needs.

The benefits and limitations of fine-tuning diffusion models

Diffusion models are a type of generative model that are trained to generate data by gradually removing noise from an image or text. Fine-tuning is a technique in machine learning where a pre-trained model is fine-tuned on a specific task. In the context of diffusion models, fine-tuning can be used to improve the performance of a pre-trained diffusion model on a specific task, such as generating images of a particular style or genre.

Here are some of the benefits of fine-tuning diffusion models:

Improved performance: Fine-tuning can be used to improve the performance of a pre-trained diffusion model on a specific task. This is because the fine-tuning process can focus on learning the specific features of the task.

Saved time and resources: Fine-tuning can be used to save time and resources, as it does not require training a model from scratch.

Transfer of knowledge: Fine-tuning can be used to transfer knowledge from one task to another. This can be useful if you have a pre-trained diffusion model that you want to use for a new task.

Here are some of the limitations of fine-tuning diffusion models:

Requires a good dataset: Fine-tuning requires a good dataset of labeled data for the specific task. If you do not have a good dataset, then fine-tuning may not be effective.

Can be time-consuming and computationally expensive: Fine-tuning can be time-consuming and computationally expensive, especially if you are using a large dataset.

Can be unstable: The fine-tuning process can be unstable, and the model can overfit the training data.

Overall, fine-tuning is a powerful technique that can be used to improve the performance of diffusion models on specific tasks. However, it is important to be aware of the limitations of fine-tuning before using it.

# Chapter 6: Deploying Diffusion Models

## How to deploy diffusion models

Diffusion models are a type of generative model that are trained to generate data by gradually removing noise from an image or text. Once a diffusion model is trained, it can be deployed to generate data.

There are several ways to deploy diffusion models:

- On-premises: The diffusion model can be deployed on-premises, meaning that it will be hosted on a server or cluster of servers in your own data center. This approach gives you the most control over the model, but it can be more expensive and time-consuming to set up.
- Cloud-based: The diffusion model can be deployed in the cloud, meaning that it will be hosted on a server or cluster of servers in a cloud provider's data center. This approach is more scalable and cost-effective than on-premises deployment, but it gives you less control over the model.
- Federated: The diffusion model can be deployed in a federated way, meaning that it will be hosted on a distributed network of servers. This approach is the most scalable and secure, but it is also the most complex to set up.

The best way to deploy a diffusion model will depend on your specific needs and requirements.

Here are some of the factors to consider when deploying diffusion models:

- The size of the model: The size of the model will affect the amount of computing resources that are needed to deploy it. A larger model will require more computing resources.
- The number of users: The number of users who will be using the model will also affect the amount of computing resources that are needed. A larger number of users will require more computing resources.
- The security requirements: The security requirements for the model will also affect the deployment options. If the model needs to be highly secure, then a federated deployment may be the best option.

Once you have decided on a deployment option, you will need to choose a deployment framework. There are several deployment frameworks available, such as TensorFlow Serving and FastAPI.

The deployment framework will provide the tools and infrastructure that you need to deploy the model. The framework will also help you to manage the model and keep it up-to-date.

Deploying diffusion models can be a complex process, but it is essential if you want to use the models to generate data in production. By following the steps outlined in this article, you can successfully deploy diffusion models and start generating data.

# Chapter 7: Ethical Considerations of Diffusion Models

## The potential risks of diffusion models

Diffusion models are a type of generative model that are trained to generate data by gradually removing noise from an image or text. Diffusion models have been shown to be capable of generating realistic and creative data, but they also pose some potential risks.
Here are some of the potential risks of diffusion models:

- Misinformation: Diffusion models can be used to generate fake images or text that can be used to spread misinformation. For example, diffusion models could be used to create fake news articles or social media posts that look like they were written by real people.
- Deepfakes: Diffusion models can be used to create deepfakes, which are videos or audio recordings that have been manipulated to make it look like someone is saying or doing something they never actually said or did. Deepfakes can be used to damage someone's reputation or to spread propaganda.
- Cyberbullying: Diffusion models can be used to create cyberbullying content, such as images or text that are designed to humiliate or harass someone. Cyberbullying can have a serious negative impact on the victim's mental health.
- Data privacy: Diffusion models are trained on large datasets of data, which can include personal information. This data could be used to track people's online activity or to create personalized advertising.
- Bias: Diffusion models can be biased, meaning that they are more likely to generate data that reflects the biases of the data they were trained on. This could lead to the generation of discriminatory or offensive content.

It is important to be aware of the potential risks of diffusion models before using them. There are a number of things that can be done to mitigate these risks, such as using certified datasets and implementing safeguards to prevent the use of diffusion models for malicious purposes.

Here are some additional considerations when using diffusion models:

- The intended use of the model: The intended use of the model will affect the risks involved. For example, a model that is used to generate images for entertainment purposes is less likely to pose a risk than a model that is used to generate images for propaganda purposes.
- The quality of the training data: The quality of the training data will affect the biases of the model. A model that is trained on a biased dataset is more likely to generate biased content.
- The security of the model: The security of the model will affect the risk of it being used for malicious purposes. A model that is not properly secured could be accessed by unauthorized users who could use it to generate harmful content.

By carefully considering the potential risks of diffusion models, we can help to ensure that they are used responsibly and ethically.

## How to mitigate the risks of diffusion models

Diffusion models are a type of generative model that are trained to generate data by gradually removing noise from an image or text. Diffusion models have been shown to be capable of generating realistic and creative data, but they also pose some potential risks.

There are a number of things that can be done to mitigate the risks of diffusion models, such as:

- Using certified datasets: Using certified datasets means that the data has been vetted for quality and bias. This will help to ensure that the model is not generating data that is harmful or misleading.

- Implementing safeguards: Implementing safeguards can help to prevent the use of diffusion models for malicious purposes. For example, a model could be designed to only generate data that is approved by a human moderator.
- Educating users: Educating users about the potential risks of diffusion models can help to prevent them from being used in harmful ways. For example, users should be aware that diffusion models can be used to generate fake images or text that could be used to spread misinformation.
- Researching new methods: Researchers are constantly developing new methods to mitigate the risks of diffusion models. For example, some researchers are working on ways to make diffusion models more transparent so that users can better understand how they work.

By taking these steps, we can help to ensure that diffusion models are used responsibly and ethically.

Here are some additional tips for mitigating the risks of diffusion models:

- Be aware of the intended use of the model: The intended use of the model will affect the risks involved. For example, a model that is used to generate images for entertainment purposes is less likely to pose a risk than a model that is used to generate images for propaganda purposes.
- Consider the quality of the training data: The quality of the training data will affect the biases of the model. A model that is trained on a biased dataset is more likely to generate biased content.
- Secure the model: The model should be secured to prevent unauthorized access. This could involve using encryption or access controls.
- Monitor the model: The model should be monitored for signs of misuse. This could involve tracking the output of the model or looking for patterns of suspicious activity.

By following these tips, we can help to mitigate the risks of diffusion models and ensure that they are used responsibly and ethically.

# The ethical implications of using diffusion models

Diffusion models are a type of generative model that are trained to generate data by gradually removing noise from an image or text. Diffusion models have been shown to be capable of generating realistic and creative data, but they also pose some ethical implications.
Here are some of the ethical implications of using diffusion models:

- Misinformation: Diffusion models can be used to generate fake images or text that can be used to spread misinformation. For example, diffusion models could be used to create fake news articles or social media posts that look like they were written by real people. This could have a negative impact on public discourse and could lead to people making decisions based on false information.
- Deepfakes: Diffusion models can be used to create deepfakes, which are videos or audio recordings that have been manipulated to make it look like someone is saying or doing something they never actually said or did. Deepfakes can be used to damage someone's reputation or to spread propaganda.
- Cyberbullying: Diffusion models can be used to create cyberbullying content, such as images or text that are designed to humiliate or harass someone. Cyberbullying can have a serious negative impact on the victim's mental health.
- Data privacy: Diffusion models are trained on large datasets of data, which can include personal information. This data could be used to track people's online activity or to create personalized advertising. This could raise concerns about privacy and security.
- Bias: Diffusion models can be biased, meaning that they are more likely to generate data that reflects the biases of the data they were trained on. This could lead to the generation of discriminatory or offensive content.

It is important to be aware of the ethical implications of using diffusion models before using them. There are a number of things that can be done to mitigate these risks, such as using certified datasets and implementing safeguards to prevent the use of diffusion models for malicious purposes.

# Chapter 8: The Mathematical Process of Diffusion

## Diffusion: The process of spreading particles from a region of high concentration to a region of low concentration

Diffusion is the process of spreading of particles from a region of high concentration to a region of low concentration. It is a fundamental process in nature and is essential for many biological and physical processes.

There are many different types of diffusion, but they all share the same basic principle. In simple terms, diffusion can be thought of as the random movement of particles. As particles move around, they tend to spread out and occupy a larger space. This process is driven by the tendency of particles to move from regions of high concentration to regions of low concentration.

The rate of diffusion is determined by a number of factors, including the temperature, the size of the particles, and the concentration gradient. The temperature affects the speed of the particles, while the size of the particles affects how easily they can move through a medium. The concentration gradient is the difference in concentration between two regions. The greater the concentration gradient, the faster the rate of diffusion.

Diffusion is a very important process in many different fields, including biology, physics, chemistry, and engineering. In biology, diffusion is essential for many processes, such as the transport of nutrients and oxygen to cells, the removal of waste products, and the spread of diseases. In physics, diffusion is used to explain the behavior of gases, liquids, and solids. In chemistry, diffusion is used to explain the rates of chemical reactions. In engineering, diffusion is used to design devices such as filters and membranes.

Diffusion is a complex process, but it is a fundamental process that is essential for many different processes in nature and technology.

# Diffusion

Diffusion is the process of particles moving from an area of high concentration to an area of low concentration. This can happen in solids, liquids, and gasses.
There are three main types of diffusion:

- Brownian motion is the random movement of particles due to the bombardment of these particles by other particles. This type of diffusion is most commonly seen in gases and liquids.

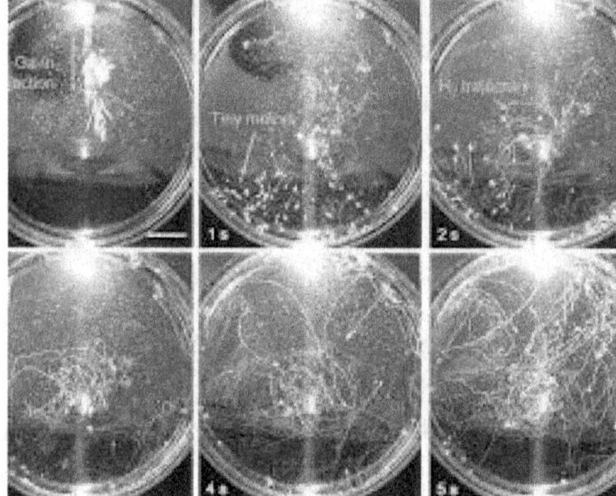

- Opens in a new window

- phys.org
- Brownian motion in a liquid

- Molecular diffusion is the movement of particles due to their own random thermal energy. This type of diffusion is most commonly seen in gasses.

- Opens in a new window

- www.slideshare.net
- Molecular diffusion in a gas
- Turbulent diffusion is the movement of particles due to the chaotic motion of fluids. This type of diffusion is most commonly seen in liquids and gasses.

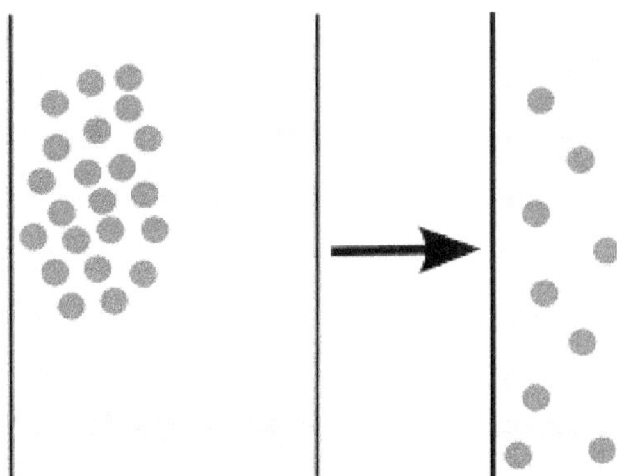

- Opens in a new window

- w en.wikipedia.org
- Turbulent diffusion in a liquid

# Brownian motion

Brownian motion is named after the Scottish botanist Robert Brown, who first observed it in 1827. He saw that pollen grains suspended in water were moving in a random, jittery motion.
Brownian motion is caused by the bombardment of the pollen grains by the water molecules. The water molecules are constantly moving, and they collide with the pollen grains, causing them to move.
The rate of Brownian motion is affected by the size of the particles, the temperature of the fluid, and the viscosity of the fluid.

# Molecular diffusion

Molecular diffusion is the movement of particles due to their own random thermal energy. The particles are constantly moving, and they collide with each other. When a particle collides with a particle of higher concentration, it is more likely to move to a region of lower concentration.
The rate of molecular diffusion is affected by the temperature of the fluid, the size of the particles, and the concentration gradient.

# Turbulent diffusion

Turbulent diffusion is the movement of particles due to the chaotic motion of fluids. This type of diffusion is most commonly seen in liquids and gases.
Turbulent diffusion is caused by the presence of eddies in the fluid. Eddies are small, swirling currents that are created by the movement of the fluid. The eddies mix the fluid, causing the particles to be distributed more evenly.
The rate of turbulent diffusion is affected by the velocity of the fluid, the size of the eddies, and the viscosity of the fluid.
Diffusion is a very important process in many different fields, such as physics, chemistry, biology, and engineering. It is used in a variety of applications, such as

the separation of mixtures, the transport of nutrients in cells, and the mixing of fluids.

## Mathematical Formulation of Diffusion

Diffusion is the process of particles moving from an area of high concentration to an area of low concentration. This can happen in solids, liquids, and gases. The mathematical formulation of diffusion is based on the diffusion equation.
The diffusion equation is a partial differential equation that describes the time evolution of the concentration of a diffusing substance. The equation is given by

$$\partial u / \partial t = D \nabla^2 u$$

where

- $u$ is the concentration of the diffusing substance
- $t$ is time
- $D$ is the diffusion coefficient, which is a measure of how fast the substance diffuses
- $\nabla$

- 2

- is the Laplacian operator, which is a mathematical operator that measures the local curvature of a function

The diffusion equation can be solved to find the concentration of the diffusing substance at any time. The solution to the diffusion equation can be used to predict how the concentration of the substance will change over time, and to design experiments to study diffusion.

The diffusion equation is a very important equation in many different fields, such as physics, chemistry, biology, and engineering. It is used in a variety of applications, such as the separation of mixtures, the transport of nutrients in cells, and the mixing of fluids.

Here is a brief explanation of the terms in the diffusion equation:

- Concentration is the amount of a substance in a given volume.
- Time is the independent variable in the diffusion equation. It represents the amount of time that has passed since the diffusion process began.
- Diffusion coefficient is a measure of how fast a substance diffuses. It is a property of the substance itself, and it is not affected by the concentration of the substance.
- Laplacian operator is a mathematical operator that measures the local curvature of a function. In the case of the diffusion equation, the Laplacian operator measures the local curvature of the concentration of the diffusing substance.

The diffusion equation is a very powerful tool for understanding and predicting diffusion. It has been used to study diffusion in a wide variety of systems, from the movement of molecules in a gas to the spread of heat in a solid.

## Different Forms of the Diffusion Equation

The diffusion equation is a partial differential equation that describes the time evolution of the concentration of a diffusing substance. The equation can be written in different forms, depending on the number of dimensions in which the diffusion is taking place.

The 1D diffusion equation is the simplest form of the diffusion equation. It describes the diffusion of a substance in one dimension, such as the diffusion of a gas in a long tube. The equation is given by

$$\partial u/\partial t = D\partial^2 u/\partial x^2$$

where

- $u$ is the concentration of the diffusing substance
- $t$ is time
- $D$ is the diffusion coefficient
- $x$ is the spatial coordinate

The 2D diffusion equation describes the diffusion of a substance in two dimensions, such as the diffusion of a liquid in a film. The equation is given by

```
∂u/∂t = D∂^2u/∂x^2 + ∂^2u/∂y^2
```

where

- $x$ and
- $y$ are the spatial coordinates

The 3D diffusion equation describes the diffusion of a substance in three dimensions, such as the diffusion of a gas in a room. The equation is given by

```
∂u/∂t = D∂^2u/∂x^2 + ∂^2u/∂y^2 + ∂^2u/∂z^2
```

where

- $x$,
- $y$, and
- $z$ are the spatial coordinates

The diffusion equation can be solved to find the concentration of the diffusing substance at any time. The solution to the diffusion equation can be used to predict how the concentration of the substance will change over time, and to design experiments to study diffusion.

The diffusion equation is a very important equation in many different fields, such as physics, chemistry, biology, and engineering. It is used in a variety of applications, such as the separation of mixtures, the transport of nutrients in cells, and the mixing of fluids.

In addition to the 1D, 2D, and 3D diffusion equations, there are also other forms of the diffusion equation. For example, the transient diffusion equation describes the diffusion of a substance in a medium that is changing over time. The anisotropic diffusion equation describes the diffusion of a substance in a medium that has different diffusion coefficients in different directions.

The choice of which form of the diffusion equation to use depends on the specific problem that is being studied.

## Meaning of the Different Terms in the Diffusion Equation

The diffusion equation is a partial differential equation that describes the time evolution of the concentration of a diffusing substance. The equation is given by

$$\partial u/\partial t = D\nabla^2 u$$

where

- $u$ is the concentration of the diffusing substance
- $t$ is time
- $D$ is the diffusion coefficient
- $\nabla$
- 2

- $\nabla^2$ is the Laplacian operator

Let's take a closer look at each of these terms.

Concentration

The concentration of a substance is the amount of the substance in a given volume. It is often expressed as a number of moles per unit volume.

Time

The time variable in the diffusion equation represents the amount of time that has passed since the diffusion process began.

Diffusion coefficient

The diffusion coefficient is a measure of how fast a substance diffuses. It is a property of the substance itself, and it is not affected by the concentration of the substance. The diffusion coefficient is typically measured in units of square meters per second.

Laplacian operator

The Laplacian operator is a mathematical operator that measures the local curvature of a function. In the case of the diffusion equation, the Laplacian operator measures the local curvature of the concentration of the diffusing substance.

The diffusion equation can be interpreted as saying that the rate of change of the concentration of the diffusing substance is proportional to the Laplacian of the concentration. In other words, the concentration of the substance will tend to spread out evenly over time.

The diffusion equation is a very important equation in many different fields, such as physics, chemistry, biology, and engineering. It is used in a variety of applications, such as the separation of mixtures, the transport of nutrients in cells, and the mixing of fluids.

# Boundary Conditions for the Diffusion Equation

The diffusion equation is a partial differential equation that describes the time evolution of the concentration of a diffusing substance. The equation is given by

$$\partial u / \partial t = D\nabla^2 u$$

where

- $u$ is the concentration of the diffusing substance
- $t$ is time
- $D$ is the diffusion coefficient
- $\nabla$

- 2

- is the Laplacian operator

The boundary conditions are the conditions that must be satisfied by the solution of the diffusion equation at the boundaries of the domain. The boundary conditions specify the values of the concentration of the diffusing substance at the boundaries. There are two main types of boundary conditions:

- Dirichlet boundary conditions specify the value of the concentration at the boundary.
- Neumann boundary conditions specify the flux of the concentration at the boundary.

Dirichlet boundary conditions are often used when the concentration of the diffusing substance is known at the boundaries. For example, if the concentration of the diffusing substance is zero at the boundaries, then this is a Dirichlet boundary condition.
Neumann boundary conditions are often used when the flux of the concentration is known at the boundaries. For example, if the flux of the diffusing substance is zero at the boundaries, then this is a Neumann boundary condition.
The choice of which type of boundary condition to use depends on the specific problem that is being studied.
Here are some examples of boundary conditions for the diffusion equation:

- A Dirichlet boundary condition:

- $u = 0$ at
- $x = 0$ and
- $x = L$.
- A Neumann boundary condition:
- $\partial u / \partial x = 0$ at
- $x = 0$ and
- $x = L$.
- A mixed boundary condition:
- $u = 0$ at
- $x = 0$ and
- $\partial u / \partial x = 0$ at
- $x = L$.

The boundary conditions must be chosen carefully in order to obtain a unique solution to the diffusion equation. If the boundary conditions are not chosen correctly, then the solution to the diffusion equation may not be physically meaningful.

# Chapter 9: Boundary Conditions

## Different Types of Boundary Conditions

Boundary conditions are constraints that are imposed on the solution of a differential equation at the boundary of the domain. They are necessary to obtain a unique solution to the differential equation.
There are many different types of boundary conditions, but some of the most common ones are:

- Dirichlet boundary conditions specify the value of the solution at the boundary.

- Neumann boundary conditions specify the normal derivative of the solution at the boundary.
- Robin boundary conditions specify a combination of the value of the solution and its normal derivative at the boundary.

Dirichlet boundary conditions are the most common type of boundary condition. They are often used when the value of the solution is known at the boundary. For example, if we know that the temperature at the boundary of a solid is 0 degrees Celsius, then we can impose a Dirichlet boundary condition of

$u = 0$ at the boundary.

Neumann boundary conditions are less common than Dirichlet boundary conditions. They are often used when the flux of the solution is known at the boundary. For example, if we know that the heat flux at the boundary of a solid is 0 watts per square meter, then we can impose a Neumann boundary condition of

$\partial u / \partial n = 0$ at the boundary.

Robin boundary conditions are a combination of Dirichlet and Neumann boundary conditions. They are often used when the solution is known at the boundary, but the flux is also known. For example, if we know that the temperature at the boundary of a solid is 0 degrees Celsius and the heat flux at the boundary is 10 watts per square meter, then we can impose a Robin boundary condition of

$ku = 0$ at the boundary, where

$k$ is a constant.

The choice of which type of boundary condition to use depends on the specific problem that is being studied.

# Imposing Boundary Conditions on the Diffusion Equation

The diffusion equation is a partial differential equation that describes the time evolution of the concentration of a diffusing substance. The equation is given by

```
∂u/∂t = D∇^2u
```

where

- $u$ is the concentration of the diffusing substance
- $t$ is time
- $D$ is the diffusion coefficient
- $\nabla$

- 2

- is the Laplacian operator

The boundary conditions are the conditions that must be satisfied by the solution of the diffusion equation at the boundaries of the domain. The boundary conditions specify the values of the concentration of the diffusing substance at the boundaries. There are two main types of boundary conditions:

- Dirichlet boundary conditions specify the value of the concentration at the boundary.
- Neumann boundary conditions specify the flux of the concentration at the boundary.

Dirichlet boundary conditions are often used when the concentration of the diffusing substance is known at the boundaries. For example, if the concentration of the diffusing substance is zero at the boundaries, then this is a Dirichlet boundary condition.
Neumann boundary conditions are often used when the flux of the concentration is known at the boundaries. For example, if the flux of the diffusing substance is zero at the boundaries, then this is a Neumann boundary condition.
To impose a Dirichlet boundary condition on the diffusion equation, we simply set the value of the solution to the specified value at the boundary. For example, if we want to impose a Dirichlet boundary condition of

$u = 0$ at

$x = 0$, then we would set

$u(0)=0$.

To impose a Neumann boundary condition on the diffusion equation, we simply set the normal derivative of the solution to the specified value at the boundary. The normal derivative is the derivative of the solution in the direction normal to the boundary. For example, if we want to impose a Neumann boundary condition of

$\partial u/\partial x =0$ at

$x =0$, then we would set

$(\partial u/\partial x)(0)=0$.

The boundary conditions must be chosen carefully in order to obtain a unique solution to the diffusion equation. If the boundary conditions are not chosen correctly, then the solution to the diffusion equation may not be physically meaningful.

Here are some examples of how to impose boundary conditions on the diffusion equation:

- Dirichlet boundary condition:
- $u =0$ at
- $x =0$ and
- $x = L$.
- Neumann boundary condition:
- $\partial u/\partial x =0$ at
- $x =0$ and
- $x = L$.
- Mixed boundary condition:
- $u =0$ at
- $x =0$ and
- $\partial u/\partial x =0$ at
- $x = L$.

# Chapter 10: Initial conditions

## Importance of Initial Conditions in the Solution of the Diffusion Equation

The diffusion equation is a partial differential equation that describes the time evolution of the concentration of a diffusing substance. The equation is given by

$$\partial u/\partial t = D\nabla^2 u$$

where

- $u$ is the concentration of the diffusing substance
- $t$ is time
- $D$ is the diffusion coefficient
- $\nabla$

- 2

- is the Laplacian operator

The initial conditions are the values of the concentration of the diffusing substance at the initial time,
$t=0$. The initial conditions are necessary to obtain a unique solution to the diffusion equation.
If the initial conditions are not specified, then the solution to the diffusion equation will be ambiguous. This is because the diffusion equation is a linear equation, and any solution of the equation can be added to any other solution of the equation.

The initial conditions can be specified in a variety of ways. For example, we can specify the concentration of the diffusing substance at all points in the domain, or we can specify the concentration of the diffusing substance at a few selected points in the domain.

The choice of how to specify the initial conditions depends on the specific problem that is being studied.

Here are some examples of how to specify initial conditions for the diffusion equation:

- Specify the concentration of the diffusing substance at all points in the domain.
- Specify the concentration of the diffusing substance at a few selected points in the domain.
- Specify the initial shape of the concentration distribution.

The initial conditions are an important part of the solution of the diffusion equation. They determine the initial state of the system, and they influence the way that the concentration of the diffusing substance evolves over time.

# Specifying Initial Conditions for the Diffusion Equation

The diffusion equation is a partial differential equation that describes the time evolution of the concentration of a diffusing substance. The equation is given by

$$\partial u/\partial t = D\nabla^2 u$$

where

- $u$ is the concentration of the diffusing substance

- $t$ is time
- $D$ is the diffusion coefficient
- $\nabla$
- 2

- is the Laplacian operator

The initial conditions are the values of the concentration of the diffusing substance at the initial time,
$t = 0$. The initial conditions are necessary to obtain a unique solution to the diffusion equation.
There are a few different ways to specify initial conditions for the diffusion equation.
Specifying the concentration at all points in the domain
This is the most general way to specify initial conditions. It is used when we know the initial concentration of the diffusing substance at all points in the domain.
Specifying the concentration at a few selected points in the domain
This is a less general way to specify initial conditions. It is used when we only know the initial concentration of the diffusing substance at a few selected points in the domain.
Specifying the initial shape of the concentration distribution
This is a way to specify initial conditions that is often used when the initial concentration of the diffusing substance has a specific shape. For example, we could specify that the initial concentration of the diffusing substance is a Gaussian distribution.
The choice of how to specify initial conditions depends on the specific problem that is being studied.
Here are some examples of how to specify initial conditions for the diffusion equation:

- Specify the concentration of the diffusing substance to be uniform throughout the domain.
- Specify the concentration of the diffusing substance to be a Gaussian distribution with mean and variance at a specific point in the domain.
- Specify the concentration of the diffusing substance to be zero at all points in the domain.

The initial conditions are an important part of the solution of the diffusion equation. They determine the initial state of the system, and they influence the way that the concentration of the diffusing substance evolves over time.

# Chapter 11: Numerical solution of the diffusion equation

The diffusion equation is a partial differential equation that describes the spread of a quantity, such as heat, concentration, or mass, over space and time. It is a fundamental equation in physics, chemistry, biology, and engineering.
The mathematical form of the diffusion equation is:

$$\partial u \partial t = D \nabla 2 u$$

where

- $u$ is the quantity that is diffusing
- $t$ is time
- $D$ is the diffusion coefficient, which is a measure of how quickly the quantity diffuses
- $\nabla$
- $2$
- is the Laplacian operator, which measures the rate of change of the quantity in space

The diffusion equation can be solved numerically using a variety of methods. Some of the most common methods are:

- Finite difference methods discretize the spatial domain into a grid and approximate the derivatives in the diffusion equation using finite difference approximations.
- Finite element methods represent the spatial domain using a mesh of elements and approximate the derivatives in the diffusion equation using integrals over the elements.
- Spectral methods use a basis of functions to represent the solution to the diffusion equation and then solve for the coefficients of the basis functions.

Each of these methods has its own advantages and disadvantages. Finite difference methods are simple to implement and can be used to solve problems with complex geometries. However, they can be inaccurate for problems with sharp gradients. Finite element methods are more accurate than finite difference methods, but they can be more computationally expensive. Spectral methods are the most accurate of the three methods, but they can also be the most computationally expensive.
The choice of which numerical method to use depends on the specific problem being solved. For simple problems, a finite difference method may be sufficient. For more complex problems, a finite element method or a spectral method may be necessary.
Here is a more detailed discussion of each of the three methods:

- Finite difference methods are the simplest and most widely used numerical methods for solving partial differential equations. They work by discretizing the spatial domain into a grid of points and then approximating the derivatives in the equation using finite difference approximations. The accuracy of the method depends on the spacing of the grid points.
- Finite element methods are more accurate than finite difference methods and are often used to solve problems with complex geometries. They work by representing the spatial domain using a mesh of elements and then approximating the derivatives in the equation using integrals over the elements. The accuracy of the method depends on the size and shape of the elements.
- Spectral methods are the most accurate of the three methods, but they can also be the most computationally expensive. They work by using a

basis of functions to represent the solution to the equation and then solving for the coefficients of the basis functions. The accuracy of the method depends on the choice of basis functions.

In addition to these three methods, there are a number of other numerical methods that can be used to solve the diffusion equation. The choice of which method to use depends on the specific problem being solved and the desired accuracy. Numerical methods are a set of techniques for solving mathematical problems by approximating them with discrete values. They are used in a wide variety of fields, including physics, engineering, economics, and statistics.
There are many different numerical methods available, each with its own advantages and disadvantages. Some of the most common methods include:

- Finite difference methods discretize the problem domain into a grid of points and then approximate the derivatives using finite difference approximations. They are simple to implement and can be used to solve problems with complex geometries. However, they can be inaccurate for problems with sharp gradients.
- Finite element methods represent the problem domain using a mesh of elements and then approximate the derivatives using integrals over the elements. They are more accurate than finite difference methods, but they can be more computationally expensive.
- Spectral methods use a basis of functions to represent the solution to the problem and then solve for the coefficients of the basis functions. They are the most accurate of the three methods, but they can also be the most computationally expensive.

The choice of which numerical method to use depends on the specific problem being solved. For simple problems, a finite difference method may be sufficient. For more complex problems, a finite element method or a spectral method may be necessary.
Here is a more detailed discussion of the advantages and disadvantages of each of the three methods:

- Finite difference methods

- Advantages:

    - Simple to implement
    - Can be used to solve problems with complex geometries

- Disadvantages:

    - Can be inaccurate for problems with sharp gradients
    - Not as accurate as finite element or spectral methods

- Finite element methods

  - Advantages:

      - More accurate than finite difference methods
      - Can be used to solve problems with complex geometries

  - Disadvantages:

      - More computationally expensive than finite difference methods
      - Can be difficult to implement for some problems

- Spectral methods

- Advantages:

    - Most accurate of the three methods
    - Can be used to solve problems with high accuracy

- Disadvantages:

    - Most computationally expensive of the three methods
    - Can be difficult to implement for some problems

In addition to these three methods, there are a number of other numerical methods that can be used to solve problems. The choice of which method to use depends on the specific problem being solved and the desired accuracy.
Here are some other factors to consider when choosing a numerical method:

- The complexity of the problem
- The accuracy required
- The computational resources available
- The expertise of the user

The best way to learn about the different numerical methods and their advantages and disadvantages is to consult a numerical methods textbook or to take a numerical methods course.

www.ingramcontent.com/pod-product-compliance
Lightning Source LLC
Chambersburg PA
CBHW071003260726